In the Year 1921

By

Kerry Butters.

In the year 1921.

Millennium: 2nd millennium

Centuries: 19th century – **20th century** – 21st century

Decades: 1890s 1900s 1910s – **1920s** – 1930s 1940s
1950s

Years: 1918 1919 1920 – **1921** – 1922 1923 1924

1921 (MCMXXI) was a common year starting on Saturday (dominical letter B) of the Gregorian calendar and a common year starting on Friday (dominical letter C) of the Julian calendar, the 1921st year of the Common Era (CE) and *Anno Domini* (AD) designations, the 921st year of the 2nd millennium, the 21st year of the 20th century, and the 2nd year of the 1920s decade. Note that the Julian day for 1921 is 13 calendar days difference, which continued to be used from 1582 until the complete conversion of the Gregorian calendar was entirely done in 1929.

Contents

Events

January

- January 1 – In American football, the University of California, Berkeley defeats Ohio State 28–0 in the Rose Bowl.
- January 2
  - The football club Cruzeiro Esporte Clube from Belo Horizonte is founded as Palestra Italia in Brazil.
  - The first religious radio broadcast is heard over station KDKA AM in Pittsburgh.
  - The Spanish liner *Santa Isabel* sinks off Villa Garcia; 244 die.
  - The De Young Museum opens in Golden Gate Park, San Francisco.
- January 20 – The British K-class submarine HMS *K5* sinks in the English Channel; all 56 on board die.
- January 21

- The Italian Communist Party is founded in Livorno.
- The Marxist Left in Slovakia and the Transcarpathian Ukraine holds its founding congress in Ľubochňa.
- Women's suffrage is attained in Sweden.
- The full-length silent comedy-drama film *The Kid*, written, produced, directed by and starring Charlie Chaplin (in his Tramp character), with Jackie Coogan, is released in the United States.
- January 25 – The Italian battleship *Leonardo da Vinci* is righted in Taranto Harbour.

February

- February 12 – Red Army invasion of Georgia: The Democratic Republic of Georgia is invaded by forces of Bolshevist Russia.
- February 20 – The Young Communist League of Czechoslovakia is founded.
- February 21 – 1921 Persian coup d'état: Rezā Khan and Zia'eddin Tabatabaee stage a coup d'état in Iran.
- February 23 – The moderately conservative public official Oscar von Sydow takes over the Swedish premiership from Baron Louis De Geer the younger.
- February 25 – Red Army invasion of Georgia: The Red Army enters the Georgian capital Tbilisi and installs a Moscow-directed communist government.

- February 27 – The International Working Union of Socialist Parties is formed in Vienna.
- February 28 – The Kronstadt rebellion is initiated by sailors of the Soviet Navy's Baltic Fleet.

March

- March – Group Settlement Scheme in Western Australia begins.
- March 1 – The city of Kiryū, located in Gunma Prefecture, Japan, is founded.
- March 4 – Warren G. Harding is inaugurated as the 29th President of the United States.
- March 5 – Irish War of Independence: Clonbanin Ambush: Irish Republican Army kills Brigadier General Cumming.
- March 6 – The Portuguese Communist Party is founded.
- March 8
  - Spanish Premier Eduardo Dato e Iradier is assassinated while exiting the parliament building in Madrid.
  - Allied forces occupy Düsseldorf, Ruhrort and Duisburg.
- March 12 – The *İstiklâl Marşı* (Independence March), the Turkish national anthem, is officially adopted.

- March 13 – Occupation of Mongolia: The Russian White Army captures Mongolia from China. Roman von Ungern-Sternberg declares himself ruler.
- March 14 – Armenian Soghomon Tehlirian assassinates Mehmed Talaat, former Interior Minister of Turkey, in Charlottenburg, Berlin.
- March 16 – Six Irish Republican Army men of the Forgotten Ten are hanged in Mountjoy Prison, Dublin.
- March 17
  - The Red Army crushes the Kronstadt rebellion and a number of sailors flee to Finland.
  - Dr. Marie Stopes opens the first birth control clinic in London, England.
  - The Second Polish Republic adopts the March Constitution.
- March 18 – The second Peace of Riga ends the Polish–Soviet War. A permanent border is established between the Polish and Soviet states.
- March 20 – Upper Silesia plebiscite votes for re-annexation to Germany.
- March 21
  - New Economic Policy starts in Soviet Russia.
  - Irish War of Independence: Headford Ambush: Irish Republican Army kills at least nine British Army troops.
- March 31 – Abkhazia becomes an autonomous republic within the Soviet Union.

April

- April – The United States Figure Skating Association is formed.
- April 11 – The Emirate of Transjordan is created, with Abdullah I as emir.
- April 14 – In Britain, labour unions for mining, railway and transportation workers call for a strike; the government threatens to call in the army.
- April 20 – Ferenc Molnár's play *Liliom* is first produced on Broadway in English.
- April 27 – The Allies of World War I reparations commission announce that Germany has to pay 132 billion gold marks ($33 trillion) in annual installments of 2.5 billion.

May

- May 1–May 7 – Jaffa riots: Riots at Jaffa in Mandatory Palestine result in 47 Jewish and 48 Arab deaths.
- May 2–July 5 – Third Silesian Uprising: Poles in Upper Silesia rise against the Germans.
- May 3 – The province of Northern Ireland is created within the United Kingdom.
- May 5 – Only thirteen spectators attend the football match between Leicester City and Stockport County, the lowest attendance in The Football League's history.

- May 6 – German-Russian Provisional Agreement signed, Germany recognised Soviet regime in Russia.
- May 14–May 15 – Major geomagnetic storm.
- May 14–May 17 – Violent anti-European riots occur in Cairo and Alexandria.
- May 16 – The Communist Party of Czechoslovakia is founded.
- May 19 – The Emergency Quota Act is passed by the United States Congress, establishing national quotas on immigration.
- May 23 – In Leipzig the Leipzig War Crimes Trials start. They will end on July 16.
- May 24 – First Northern Ireland general election for the new Parliament of Northern Ireland is held.
- May 26 – A general strike begins in Norway.
- May 31 – Tulsa race riot begins in Tulsa, Oklahoma. The official death toll is 39, but later investigations suggest the actual toll may be much higher.

June

- June 21 – International Hydrographic Bureau (IHB) established as an agency of the League of Nations; continues in this form until April 19, 1946.
- June 27 – The first signings of Treaty 11, an agreement between George V, King of Canada, and various Canadian First Nations, are conducted at Fort Providence.

- June 28 – The Constitutional Assembly of the Kingdom of Serbs, Croats and Slovenes passes the Vidovdan Constitution, despite a boycott of the vote by the communists, and Croat and Slovene parties.
- June 30 – The death penalty is abolished in Sweden.

July

- July 1
  - The Communist Party of China (CPC) is founded.
  - A coal strike ends in England.
- July 2 – U.S. President Warren Harding signs a joint congressional resolution declaring an end to America's state of war with Germany, Austria and Hungary.
- July 4 – A new conservative government is formed in Italy by Ivanoe Bonomi.
- July 11
  - The Irish War of Independence (aka the Anglo-Irish War) comes to a halt after a truce is signed between the belligerents.
  - The Red Army captures Mongolia from the White Army and establishes the Mongolian People's Republic.
- July 14 – A Massachusetts jury finds Nicola Sacco and Bartolomeo Vanzetti guilty of first degree murder following a widely publicized trial.

- July 17 – The Republic of Mirdita is proclaimed near the Albanian-Serbian border with Yugoslav support.
- July 18 – The first BCG vaccination against tuberculosis is given.
- July 21 – Rif War – Battle of Annual: Spanish troops are dealt a crushing defeat at the hands of Abd el-Krim.
- July 22 – The Anglo-Irish truce, agreed 10 days earlier, is officially declared in London.
- July 23 – The Communist Party of China (CPC) launched the first time of founding National Congress, Communist party in China are established.
- July 26 – U.S. President Warren G. Harding receives Princess Fatima of Afghanistan and Stanley Clifford Weyman.
- July 27 – Researchers at the University of Toronto led by biochemist Frederick Banting announce the discovery of the hormone insulin.
- July 29 – Adolf Hitler becomes Führer of the Nazi Party.

August

- August – The United States formally ends World War I.
- August 5 – The first radio baseball game is broadcast; Harold Arlin announces the Pirates-Phillies game

from Forbes Field over Westinghouse KDKA, in Pittsburgh.

- August 11 – The temperature reaches 39 degrees Celsius in Breslau; the heat wave continues elsewhere in Europe as well.
- August 23 – King Faisal I of Iraq is crowned in Baghdad.
- August 24 – R38-class airship ZR-2 explodes on her fourth test flight near Kingston upon Hull, England, killing 44 of the 49 Anglo-American crew on board.
- August 25 – Franklin Roosevelt, 39, is diagnosed with poliomyelitis following a two-week illness characterized by paralysis and fevers. He would be permanently disabled after this illness.
- August 26
  - Rising prices cause major riots in Munich.
  - The assassination of German politician Matthias Erzberger causes the government to declare martial law.

September

- September 1 – Poplar Strike in London: Nine members of the Poplar borough council are arrested.
- September 7 – In Atlantic City, New Jersey, the first Miss America Pageant is held.
- September 8 – Sixteen-year-old Margaret Gorman wins the Atlantic City Pageant's Golden Mermaid

trophy; pageant officials later dub her the first Miss America.

- September 12 – The Lotta Svärd women's paramilitary auxiliary is founded in Finland.
- September 13 – White Castle hamburger restaurant opens in Wichita, Kansas, the foundation of the world's first fast food chain.
- September 21 – The Oppau explosion occurs at BASF's nitrate factory in Oppau, Germany; 500 – 600 are killed.

October

- October 5 – The first broadcast of a World Series game on the radio, by Newark, New Jersey, station WJZ; Pittsburgh station KDKA; and a group of other commercial and amateur stations throughout the eastern United States.
- October 8 – The first Sweetest Day is staged in Cleveland, Ohio.
- October 10 – Teaching at the University of Szeged starts in the Kingdom of Hungary.
- October 13 –
  - The Treaty of Kars is signed between the Grand National Assembly of Turkey and the Soviet Socialist Republics of Armenia, Azerbaijan and Georgia, establishing the boundaries between Turkey and the states of the south Caucasus.

- Swedish Social Democratic party leader Hjalmar Branting becomes yet again Prime Minister, after strong general election gains for his party.
- October 19 – 'Bloody Night' (*Noite Sangrenta*): A massacre in Lisbon claims the lives of Portuguese Prime-Minister António Granjo and other politicians.
- October 21
  - A peace conference between Ireland and the United Kingdom begins in London.
  - George Melford's wildly successful silent film *The Sheik*, which will propel its leading actor Rudolph Valentino to international stardom, is premiered in Los Angeles.
- October 24 – The Spanish Army defeats rifkabyl rebels in Morocco.
- October 29 – In the United States
  - Construction of the Link River Dam, a part of the Klamath Project in Oregon, is completed.
  - Centre College's American football team, led by quarterback Bo McMillin, defeats Harvard University 6–0 to break Harvard's five-year winning streak. For decades afterward, this is called "football's upset of the century."

November

- November 4 – After a speech by Adolf Hitler in the Hofbräuhaus in Munich (Germany), members of the *Sturmabteilung* ("brownshirts") physically assault his opposition.
- November 9
    - The National Fascist Party (*Partito Nazionale Fascista* or PNF) is founded in Italy.
    - Albert Einstein is awarded the Nobel Prize in Physics for his work with the photoelectric effect.
    - Riots in Reykjavík injure most of the small police force.
- November 11 – During an Armistice Day ceremony at Arlington National Cemetery, the Tomb of the Unknown Soldier is dedicated by Warren G. Harding, President of the United States.
- November 14 – The Spanish Communist Party is founded.
- November 23 – The Sheppard–Towner Act is signed by President Harding, providing federal funding for maternity and child care.
- Undated – Hyperinflation rampant in Germany, where 263 marks are now needed to buy a single American dollar, more than 20 times greater than the 12 marks needed in April 1919.

December

- December 1 – Rising prices cause riots in Vienna.
- December 6
  - The Anglo-Irish Treaty establishing the Irish Free State, an independent nation incorporating 26 of Ireland's 32 counties, is signed in London.
  - Agnes Macphail becomes the first woman to be elected to the Canadian Parliament.
- December 13 – In the Four-Power Treaty on Insular Possessions, Japan, the United States, United Kingdom, and France agree to recognize the status quo in the Pacific.
- December 23 – Visva-Bharati College is founded by Rabindranath Tagore in Santiniketan, Bengal Presidency, British India.
- December 29 – William Lyon Mackenzie King becomes Canada's tenth prime minister.

Date unknown

- Russian famine: Roughly 5,000,000 people die.
- Jewish immigration to Palestine grows rapidly after the United States drastically limits immigration from Eastern Europe.
- Regular radio broadcasting services begin in Italy.

- Edward Harper, the "father of broadcasting" in Ceylon, arrives in Colombo to take up his post as Chief Engineer of the Ceylon Telegraph Department.
- The vibraphone in its original form is invented in the United States.
- E. W. Scripps and William Emerson Ritter found *Science Service*, later renamed Society for Science and the Public, in the United States with the goal of keeping the public informed of scientific developments.
- The Sauerländer Heimatbund is founded in Meschede, Germany.
- Weimar Republic makes its first payment of reparations.

Births

January

Friedrich Dürrenmatt

Donna Reed

Carol Channing

- January 1
  - César Baldaccini, French sculptor (d. 1998)
  - Doris Tetzlaff, American female professional baseball player (d. 1998)
- January 5
  - Friedrich Dürrenmatt, Swiss writer (d. 1990)
  - Jean, Grand Duke of Luxembourg
- January 9
  - Fraser Barron, New Zealand bomber pilot during WWII (d. 1944)
  - Ágnes Keleti, Hungarian artistic gymnast
  - Lister Sinclair, Canadian broadcaster and playwright (d. 2006)

- January 10 – Rodger Ward, American race car driver (d. 2004)
- January 14 – Murray Bookchin, American libertarian socialist (d. 2006)
- January 19 – Patricia Highsmith, American author (d. 1995)
- January 21 – Howard Unruh, American spree killer (d. 2009)
- January 26 – Akio Morita, Japanese businessman, co-founder of Sony (d. 1999)
- January 27 – Donna Reed, American actress (d. 1986)
- January 31
  - Carol Channing, American actress
  - Mario Lanza, American tenor and actor (d. 1959)

February

Lana Turner

Betty Hutton

- February 1 – Peter Sallis, English actor (*Last of the Summer Wine*; *Wallace and Gromit*)
- February 4 – Betty Friedan, American feminist (d. 2006)
- February 5
  - John Pritchard, English conductor (d. 1989)
  - Sir Ken Adam, German-born British production designer (d. 2016)
- February 7 – Nexhmije Hoxha, widow of Enver Hoxha
- February 8
  - Betsy Jochum, American female baseball player
  - Lana Turner, American actress (d. 1995)
- February 11 – Lloyd Bentsen, American politician (d. 2006)
- February 14 – Hugh Downs, American game show host and journalist
- February 16
  - Hua Guofeng, former Chairman of the Communist Party of China and Premier of China (d. 2008)
  - Vera-Ellen, American actress and dancer (d.1981)
- February 17 – Muriel Coben, Canadian professional baseball and curling player (d. 1979)
- February 20 – "Nature Boy" Rogers, American professional wrestler (d. 1992)
- February 22
  - Wayne C. Booth, American literary critic (d. 2005)

- ○ Giulietta Masina, Italian actress (d. 1994)
- February 24 – Abe Vigoda, American actor (d. 2016)
- February 25 – Pierre Laporte, Canadian statesman (d. 1970)
- February 26 – Betty Hutton, American actress (d. 2007)
- February 28 – Pierre Clostermann, French World War II pilot (d. 2006)

March

King Fahd of Saudi Arabia

- March 1
  - ○ Jack Clayton, British film director (d. 1995)
  - ○ Terence Cardinal Cooke, American Roman Catholic prelate (d. 1983)
  - ○ Richard Wilbur, American poet
- March 2 – Robert Simpson, English composer (d. 1997)
- March 3
  - ○ Diana Barrymore, American actress (d. 1960)
  - ○ Paul Guimard, French writer (d. 2004)
- March 4

- o Halim El-Dabh, Egyptian-born U.S. composer, performer, ethnomusicologist and educator
  - o Joan Greenwood, British actress (d. 1987)
- March 5 – Elmer Valo, Czechoslovakia-born Major League Baseball player (d. 1998)
- March 8 – Alan Hale, Jr., American actor (*Gilligan's Island*) (d. 1990)
- March 11
  - o Frank Harary, American mathematician (d. 2005)
  - o Astor Piazzolla, Argentine tango composer, bandoneon player and arranger (d. 1992)
- March 12
  - o Gianni Agnelli, Italian auto executive (d. 2003)
  - o Gordon MacRae, American singer and actor (d. 1986)
- March 13
  - o Al Jaffee, American cartoonist (*MAD Magazine*)
  - o Cyril Poole, English cricketer (d. 1996)
- March 16 – King Faud of Saudi Arabia (d. 2005)
- March 14 – Lis Hartel, Danish equestrian athlete (d. 2009)
- March 17 – Meir Amit, Israeli politician and general (d. 2009)
- March 19 – Tommy Cooper, Welsh prop comedian and magician (d.1984)
- March 20 – Alfréd Rényi, Hungarian mathematician (d. 1970)

- March 21 – Arthur Grumiaux, Belgian violinist (d. 1986)
- March 24
    - Wilson Harris, Guyanese writer
    - Vasily Smyslov, Soviet chess player (d. 2010)
- March 25 – Simone Signoret, French actress (d. 1985)
- March 28 – Dirk Bogarde, English actor (d. 1999)

April

Yitzhak Navon

Peter Ustinov

- April 1 – Beau Jack, American boxer (d. 2000)
- April 3
    - Robert Karvelas, American actor (d. 1991)
    - Jan Sterling, American actress (d. 2004)
- April 8 – Franco Corelli, Italian opera singer (d. 2003)

- April 9
  - Frankie Thomas, American actor (d. 2006)
  - Yitzhak Navon, Israeli politician (d. 2015)
- April 10
  - Chuck Connors, American basketball and baseball player turned actor (d.1992)
  - Sheb Wooley, American actor, singer (d. 2003)
- April 14 – Thomas Schelling, American economist, Nobel Prize laureate
- April 15 – Georgy Beregovoy, Soviet cosmonaut (d. 1995)
- April 16 – Peter Ustinov, English actor and director (d. 2004)
- April 17 – Sergio Sollima, Italian director (d. 2015)
- April 19 – Roberto Tucci, Italian cardinal and theologian (d. 2015)
- April 22 – Vivian Dandridge, African-American actress (d.1991)
- April 23
  - Judy Agnew, Second Lady of the United States (d. 2012)
  - Janet Blair, American actress (d. 2007)
  - Warren Spahn, American baseball player (d. 2003)
- April 25 – Karel Appel, Dutch painter (d. 2006)
- April 26 – Jimmy Giuffre, American jazz musician (d. 2008)

- April 27 – Hans-Joachim Kulenkampff, German television host and entertainer (d. 1998)
- April 30
  - Dottie Green, American professional baseball player (d. 1992)
  - Tove Maës, Danish actress (d. 2010)

May

- May 2 – Satyajit Ray, Indian filmmaker (d. 1992)
- May 5 – Arthur Leonard Schawlow, American physicist, Nobel Prize laureate (d. 1999)
- May 6 – Erich Fried, Austrian author (d. 1988)
- May 9
  - Sophie Scholl, Anti-Nazi Resistance fighter (d. 1943)
  - Mona Van Duyn, American poet (d. 2004)
- May 11 – Hildegard Hamm-Brücher, German politician
- May 12
  - Joseph Beuys, German artist (d.1986)
  - Farley Mowat, Canadian writer and naturalist (d. 2014)
- May 14 – Richard Deacon, American actor (d. 1984)
- May 16 – Harry Carey, Jr., American actor (d. 2012)
- May 17 – Dennis Brain, English musician (d. 1957)
- May 18 – Sir Michael A. Epstein, British medical researcher

- May 19 – Karel van het Reve, Dutch writer (d. 1999)
- May 20
  - Wolfgang Borchert, German writer (d. 1947)
  - Hal Newhouser, baseball player (d. 1998)
- May 21
  - Andrei Sakharov, Soviet physicist and human rights activist, recipient of the Nobel Peace Prize (which he declined) (d. 1989)
  - Prabhat Ranjan Sarkar, Indian philosopher, author of the socio-economic Progressive Utilization Theory (d. 1990)
- May 23
  - James Blish, American science fiction author (d. 1975)
  - Humphrey Lyttelton, British jazz musician and radio personality (d. 2008)
- May 25
  - Hal David, American songwriter and lyricist (d. 2012)
  - James C. Quayle, American newspaper publisher (d. 2000)
  - Jack Steinberger, German-born physicist, Nobel Prize laureate
- May 26 – Stan Mortensen, English footballer (d. 1991)
- May 28
  - Tom Uren, Australian soldier and politician (d. 2015)
  - Heinz G. Konsalik, German author (d. 1999)

- May 29
    - Norman Hetherington, Australian puppeteer & artist (d. 2010)
    - Clifton James, American character actor

June

Alexis Smith

Jane Russell

- June 1 – Nelson Riddle, American bandleader (d. 1985)
- June 3
    - Forbes Carlile, Australian athlete
    - John Shelton Wilder, American politician, former Lieutenant Governor of Tennessee (d. 2010)&
- June 7 – Bernard Lown, American medical innovator; awarded the Nobel Peace Prize
- June 8

- Alexis Smith, Canadian-born American actress (d. 1993)
- Suharto, former President of Indonesia (d. 2008)
- June 9 – Margaret Danhauser, American female professional baseball player (d. 1987)
- June 10 – Prince Philip, Duke of Edinburgh, consort of Elizabeth II
- June 12
  - Christopher Derrick, British writer (d. 2007)
  - Johan Witteveen, Dutch politician and economist, 5th Managing Director of the IMF
- June 13 – Nancy Warren, American female professional baseball player (d. 2001)
- June 15 – Erroll Garner, American jazz musician (d. 1977)
- June 19 – Louis Jourdan, French actor (d. 2015)
- June 21 – Jane Russell, American actress (d. 2011)
- June 22 – Ralph K. Hofer, American fighter pilot (d. 1942)
- June 25 – Celia Franca, Canadian ballet dancer (d. 2007)
- June 26 – Violette Szabo, French World War II heroine (d. 1945)
- June 28 – P. V. Narasimha Rao, Prime Minister of India (d. 2004)

July

Gérard Debreu

Nancy Reagan

- July 3 – Levi Yitzchak Horowitz, Hasidic rebbe (d. 2009)
- July 4
    - Gérard Debreu, French economist, Nobel Prize laureate (d. 2004)
    - Tibor Varga, Hungarian violinist and conductor (d. 2003)
- July 6 – Nancy Davis Reagan, actress; First Lady of the United States, wife of U.S. President Ronald Reagan (d. 2016)
- July 10
    - Harvey Ball, American designer (d. 2001)

- Eunice Kennedy Shriver, member of the Kennedy family (d. 2009)
- July 11 – Ilse Werner, German actress (d. 2005)
- July 13 – Friedrich Peter, Austrian politician (d. 2005)
- July 14
    - Leon Garfield, English writer (d. 1996)
    - Geoffrey Wilkinson, English chemist, Nobel Prize laureate (d. 1996)
- July 15 – Robert Bruce Merrifield, American chemist, Nobel Prize laureate (d. 2006)
- July 16 – Boscoe Holder, Trinidadian artist (d. 2007)
- July 17
    - Hannah Szenes, Hungarian World War II heroine (d. 1944)
    - František Zvarík, Slovakian actor (d. 2008)
- July 18
    - Aaron T. Beck, American psychiatrist
    - John Glenn, American astronaut and former U.S. Senator
    - Richard Leacock, Documentary filmmaker, Pioneer of Cinéma Vérité (d. 2011)
- July 19 – Rosalyn Sussman Yalow, American physicist, recipient of the Nobel Prize in Physiology or Medicine (d. 2011)
- July 22 – William Roth, U.S. Senator (d. 2003)
- July 24 – Billy Taylor, American jazz musician (d. 2010)

- July 30 – Grant Johannesen, American concert pianist (d. 2005)

August

Esther Williams

Gene Roddenberry

- August 3 – Richard Adler, American Broadway composer (d. 2012)
- August 4 – Maurice Richard, Canadian hockey player (d. 2000)
- August 8 – Esther Williams, American swimmer and actress (d. 2013)
- August 9
  - Ernest Angley, American televangelist, author and station owner

- J. James Exon, Governor of Nebraska and U.S. Senator (d. 2005)
  - Patricia Marmont, American actress, daughter of Percy Marmont
- August 10 – Yuki Shimoda, American actor (d. 1981)
- August 13 – Barney Liddell, American musician (d. 2003)
- August 18 – Zdzisław Żygulski, Jr., Polish art historian (d. 2015)
- August 19 – Gene Roddenberry, American television producer (d.1991)
- August 21 – John Osteen, American televangelist (d. 1999)
- August 23 – Kenneth Arrow, American economist, Nobel Prize laureate
- August 25
  - Monty Hall, Canadian-born American game show host
  - Brian Moore, Northern Irish-born Canadian writer (d. 1999)
- August 26
  - Shimshon Amitsur, Israeli mathematician and Israel Prize recipient (d. 1994)
  - Benjamin Bradlee, American journalist, executive editor of *The Washington Post* (d. 2014)
- August 27 – Georg Alexander, Duke of Mecklenburg, head of the House of Mecklenburg-Strelitz (d. 1996)
- August 28

- John Herbert Chapman, Canadian physicist (d. 1979)
- Nancy Kulp, American actress (d. 1991)
- Lidia Gueiler Tejada, President of Bolivia (d. 2011)

September

Stanisław Lem

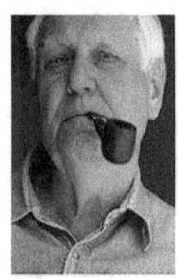

Miklós Jancsó

Deborah Kerr

- September 2 – Josephine Lenard, American professional baseball player (d. 2007)
- September 3 – Thurston Dart, English harpsichordist and conductor (d. 1971)
- September 8
  ○ Mosie Lister, American singer (d. 2015)
  ○ Harry Secombe, Welsh entertainer (d. 2001)
- September 12
  ○ Stanisław Lem, Polish science fiction writer (d. 2006)
  ○ Frank McGee, American television personality (d. 1974)
- September 13 – Sergey Nepobedimy, Soviet rocket weaponry designer (d. 2014)
- September 14 – Dario Vittori, Argentine actor (d. 2001)
- September 15 – Norma MacMillan, voice actress (d. 2001)
- September 24
  ○ Jim McKay, American sportscaster (d. 2008)
  ○ Charlene Pryer, American professional baseball player (d. 1999)
- September 27
  ○ Miklós Jancsó, Hungarian film director (d. 2014)
  ○ Bernard Waber, American children's author (d. 2013)
- September 30
  ○ Deborah Kerr, Scottish actress (d. 2007)

- Jorge Loring Miró, Spanish Jesuit priest, public speaker and author (d. 2013)

October

- October 2 – Robert Runcie, Archbishop of Canterbury (d. 2000)
- October 5 – Bill Willis, American football player (d. 2007)
- October 7 – Tommy Farrell, American supporting actor and comedian (d. 2004)
- October 8 – Abraham Sarmiento, Filipino Supreme Court jurist (d. 2010)
- October 11 – Shaw McCutcheon, American cartoonist
- October 13
  - Enrico Cocozza, Scottish filmmaker (d. 2009)
  - Yves Montand, French singer and actor (d. 1991)
- October 14
  - José Arraño Acevedo, Chilean historian (d. 2009)
  - Thomaz Soares da Silva, Brazilian football player (d. 2002)
- October 17 – Maria Gorokhovskaya, Soviet gymnast (d. 2001)
- October 18
  - Jerry Cooke, American photographer (d. 2005)
  - Jesse Helms, U.S. Senator from North Carolina (d. 2008)
- October 19

- George Nader, American actor (d. 2002)
  - Gunnar Nordahl, Swedish footballer (d. 1995)
- October 21
  - Malcolm Arnold, British music composer (d. 2006)
  - Ingrid van Houten-Groeneveld, Dutch astronomer (d. 2015)
- October 22 – Georges Brassens, French singer-songwriter (d.1981)
- October 23 – André Turcat, French aviator and first pilot of Concorde (d.2016)
- October 24 – Sena Jurinac, Bosnian operatic soprano (d. 2011)
- October 25 – King Michael I of Romania
- October 26 – Frances Scott Fitzgerald, writer; daughter of F. Scott and Zelda Fitzgerald (d. 1986)

November

Charles Bronson

Rodney Dangerfield

Jackie Stallone

- November 3 – Charles Bronson, American actor (d. 2003)
- November 5 – Princess Fawzia Fuad of Egypt (d. 2013)
- November 6 – James Jones, American writer (d. 1977)
- November 8 – Gene Saks, American actor and film director (d. 2015)
- November 10 – Owen Bush, American actor (d. 2001)
- November 11
    - Molly Dodd, American actress (d. 1981)
    - Ron Greenwood, English football manager (d. 2006)

- November 13 – Joonas Kokkonen, Finnish composer (d. 1996)
- November 14 – Brian Keith, American actor (d. 1997)
- November 17 – Albert Bertelsen, Danish artist
- November 20 – Dan Frazer, American actor (d. 2011)
- November 22 – Rodney Dangerfield, American actor and comedian (d. 2004)
- November 23 – Fred Buscaglione, Italian singer and actor (d. 1960)
- November 27 – Alexander Dubček, Slovak politician and First Secretary of the Central Committee of the Communist Party of Czechoslovakia (d. 1992)
- November 29 – Jackie Stallone, American astrologer and mother of Sylvester Stallone

December

- December 2 – Carlo Furno, Italian cardinal (d. 2015)
- December 3 – Phyllis Curtin, American soprano
- December 4 – Deanna Durbin, Canadian singer (d. 2013)
- December 5 – Alvy Moore, American actor (d. 1997)
- December 6 – Otto Graham, American football player (d. 2003)
- December 11 – Liz Smith, British actress
- December 19 – Blaže Koneski, Macedonian poet and linguist (d.1993)
- December 21

- ○ Alicia Alonso, Cuban ballerina
- ○ Luigi Creatore, American songwriter and record producer (d. 2015)
- December 23 – Marge Callaghan, Canadian female professional baseball player
- December 26 – Steve Allen, American actor, composer, comedian, and author (d. 2000)
- December 31 – Maurice Yaméogo, President of Upper Volta (d. 1993)

Deaths

January–June

Theobald von Bethmann-Hollweg

- January 1 – Theobald von Bethmann-Hollweg, former Chancellor of Germany (b. 1856)
- January 18 – Adolf von Hildebrand, German sculptor (b. 1847)
- January 29 – H. G. Haugan, Norwegian-born American railroad and banking executive (b. 1840)

- February 2 – Antonio Jacobsen, maritime artist (b. 1850)
- February 7 – John J. Gardner, American politician (b. 1845)
- February 8
  - Peter Kropotkin, Russian anarchist (b. 1842)
  - George Formby Snr, English entertainer (b. 1876)
- February 26 – Carl Menger, Austrian economist (b. 1840)
- February 27 – Schofield Haigh, English cricketer (b. 1871)
- March 1 – King Nicholas I of Montenegro (b. 1841)
- March 8 – Eduardo Dato, Prime Minister of Spain (b. 1856) (assassinated)
- March 29 – John Burroughs, American naturalist and essayist (b. 1837)
- April 1 – Edmund Poë, British admiral (b. 1849)
- April 11 – Augusta Victoria of Schleswig-Holstein, last German Empress, wife of Wilhelm II (b. 1858)
- April 17 – Manwel Dimech, Maltese philosopher and social reformer (b. 1860)
- April 21 – Tom O'Brien, American Major League Baseball player (b. 1860)
- April 27 – Arthur Mold, English cricketer (b. 1863)
- May 5 – Alfred Hermann Fried, Austrian writer and pacifist, recipient of the Nobel Peace Prize (b. 1864)
- May 12 – Emilia Pardo Bazán, Spanish writer (b. 1851)
- May 19

- Edward Douglass White, 9th Chief Justice of the United States (b. 1845)
  - Michael Llewelyn Davies, one of the 'Lost Boys' for the Peter Pan book (b. 1900)
- May 25 – Émile Combes, French politician, former Prime Minister (b. 1835)
- June 5 – Georges Feydeau, French playwright (b. 1862)
- June 18 – Eduardo Acevedo Díaz, Uruguayan writer (b. 1851)
- June 26 – Alfred Percy Sinnett, British writer (b. 1840)
- June 28 – Gyorche Petrov, Macedonian and Bulgarian revolutionary (b. 1865) (assassinated)
- June 29
  - Lady Randolph Churchill, mother of Winston Churchill (b. 1854)
  - Otto Seeck, German classical historian (b. 1850)

July–December

Enrico Caruso

Engelbert Humperdinck

- July 1 – Maurice Bailloud, French general (b. 1847)
- July 26 – Howard Vernon, Australian actor (b. 1848)
- August 2 – Enrico Caruso, Italian tenor (b. 1873)
- August 7 – Alexander Blok, Russian poet (b. 1880)
- August 8 – Juhani Aho, Finnish author and journalist (b. 1861)
- August 16 – Peter I of Serbia, King of Yugoslavia (b. 1844)
- August 19 – Georges Darien, French writer (b. 1862)
- August 31 – Karl von Bülow, German field marshal (b. 1846)
- September 2 – Henry Austin Dobson, English poet (b. 1840)
- September 7 – Alfred William Rich, English watercolour painter (b. 1856)
- September 9 – Virginia Rappe, American model and actress (b. 1895)
- September 11
  - Prince Louis of Battenberg, British naval officer and German prince (b. 1854)

- ○ Subramania Bharati, Tamil poet (b. 1882)
- September 27 – Engelbert Humperdinck, German composer (b. 1854)
- October 12 – Philander C. Knox, American politician (b. 1853)
- October 17 – Yaa Asantewaa, Asante warrior queen (b. c. 1840)
- October 18 – Ludwig III of Bavaria, last king of Bavaria (b. 1845)

John Boyd Dunlop

- October 23 – John Boyd Dunlop, Irish Scottish-born inventor and veterinary surgeon (b. 1840)
- October 25 – Bat Masterson, American gunfighter (b. 1853)
- November 4 – Hara Takashi, 19th Prime Minister of Japan (b. 1856) (assassinated)
- November 12 – Fernand Khnopff, Belgian painter (b. 1858)
- November 14 – Isabel, Princess Imperial of Brazil, daughter of Emperor Pedro II of Brazil (b. 1846)

- November 20 – Christina Nilsson, Swedish operatic soprano (b. 1843)
- November 26 – Charles Whittlesey, United States Army officer, commander of the "Lost Battalion" in World War I (suicide) (b. 1884)
- November 27 – Douglas Colin Cameron, Canadian politician (b. 1854)
- November 28 – `Abdu'l-Bahá, Persian religious leader (b. 1844)
- December 10 – George Ashlin, Irish architect (b. 1837)
- December 12 – Henrietta Swan Leavitt, American astronomer (b. 1868)
- December 16 – Camille Saint-Saëns, French composer (b. 1835)
- December 20
  - Dmitri Parsky, Russian general (b. 1866)
  - Julius Richard Petri, German microbiologist (b. 1852)
- December 31 – Boies Penrose, U.S. Senator from Pennsylvania (b. 1860)

Nobel Prizes

- Physics – Albert Einstein
- Chemistry – Frederick Soddy
- Medicine – not awarded
- Literature – Anatole France
- Peace – Karl Hjalmar Branting, Christian Lous Lange

In the News

Adolf Hitler becomes Chairman of the Nazi Party in his rise to power and prominence in Germany.

Tomb of the Unknowns is dedicated in Arlington National Cemetery.

One of the worst famines in modern times, grips Russia due to the failure of crops.

Chanel Number 5 Perfume is introduced.

Franklin D. Roosevelt, at 39 years old, contracts Polio.

Sleeping Sickness claims nearly 1,000 lives in the US.

More and more tests and advancements are being made that will later provide the basis for television technology that will be used in millions of homes.

1921 Calendar.

January 1921

Sun	Mon	Tue	Wed	Thu	Fri	Sat
						1
2	3	4	5	6	7	8
9	10	11	12	13	14	15
16	17	18	19	20	21	22
23	24	25	26	27	28	29
30	31					

February 1921

Sun	Mon	Tue	Wed	Thu	Fri	Sat
		1	2	3	4	5
6	7	8	9	10	11	12
13	14	15	16	17	18	19
20	21	22	23	24	25	26
27	28					

March 1921

Sun	Mon	Tue	Wed	Thu	Fri	Sat
		1	2	3	4	5
6	7	8	9	10	11	12
13	14	15	16	17	18	19
20	21	22	23	24	25	26
27	28	29	30	31		

April 1921

Sun	Mon	Tue	Wed	Thu	Fri	Sat
					1	2
3	4	5	6	7	8	9
10	11	12	13	14	15	16
17	18	19	20	21	22	23
24	25	26	27	28	29	30

May 1921

Sun	Mon	Tue	Wed	Thu	Fri	Sat
1	2	3	4	5	6	7
8	9	10	11	12	13	14
15	16	17	18	19	20	21
22	23	24	25	26	27	28
29	30	31				

June 1921

Sun	Mon	Tue	Wed	Thu	Fri	Sat
			1	2	3	4
5	6	7	8	9	10	11
12	13	14	15	16	17	18
19	20	21	22	23	24	25
26	27	28	29	30		

July 1921

Sun	Mon	Tue	Wed	Thu	Fri	Sat
					1	2
3	4	5	6	7	8	9
10	11	12	13	14	15	16
17	18	19	20	21	22	23
24	25	26	27	28	29	30
31						

August 1921

Sun	Mon	Tue	Wed	Thu	Fri	Sat
	1	2	3	4	5	6
7	8	9	10	11	12	13
14	15	16	17	18	19	20
21	22	23	24	25	26	27
28	29	30	31			

September 1921

Sun	Mon	Tue	Wed	Thu	Fri	Sat
				1	2	3
4	5	6	7	8	9	10
11	12	13	14	15	16	17
18	19	20	21	22	23	24
25	26	27	28	29	30	

October 1921

Sun	Mon	Tue	Wed	Thu	Fri	Sat
						1
2	3	4	5	6	7	8
9	10	11	12	13	14	15
16	17	18	19	20	21	22
23	24	25	26	27	28	29
30	31					

November 1921

Sun	Mon	Tue	Wed	Thu	Fri	Sat
		1	2	3	4	5
6	7	8	9	10	11	12
13	14	15	16	17	18	19
20	21	22	23	24	25	26
27	28	29	30			

December 1921

Sun	Mon	Tue	Wed	Thu	Fri	Sat
				1	2	3
4	5	6	7	8	9	10
11	12	13	14	15	16	17
18	19	20	21	22	23	24
25	26	27	28	29	30	31

www.ingramcontent.com/pod-product-compliance
Lightning Source LLC
Chambersburg PA
CBHW071138280526
45787CB00003B/1327